SEE HOW
I GROW

SEE HOW
I GROW

written by
ANGELA WILKES

DORLING KINDERSLEY

LONDON • NEW YORK • STUTTGART

A DORLING KINDERSLEY BOOK

Editor Claire Bampton **Designer** Jane Bull
Assistant Designer Susan St. Louis **Production** Catherine Semark
Managing editor Sophie Mitchell **Managing art editor** Miranda Kennedy
U.S. Assistant editor Lara Tankel

First American Edition, 1994
2 4 6 8 10 9 7 5 3 1
Published in the United States by
Dorling Kindersley, Inc., 232 Madison Avenue
New York, New York 10016

Distributed by Houghton Mifflin Company, Boston.
Library of Congress Cataloging-in-Publication Data
Wilkes, Angela.
See how I grow / by Angela Wilkes. – 1st American ed.
p. cm.
ISBN 1-56458-464-X
1. Infants – Growth – Juvenile literature. 2. Infants – Development
– Juvenile literature. [1. Growth. 2. Babies.] I. Title.
RJ134.W55 1994 612.6'54 – dc20   93-27039 CIP AC
Color reproduction by Colourscan, Singapore
Printed and bound in Italy by L.E.G.O.

CONTENTS

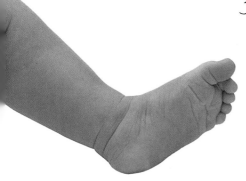

Where am I?

I was just born. For nine months I have been inside my mommy, but now I am in this strange new world. I spend most of my time asleep.

I am four days old. See how tiny I am next to my basket.

I spend about 18 hours a day fast asleep.

Time to wake up. Where am I?

I'm hungry and start to cry for food.

Mommy picks
me up. When
she holds me,
I feel warm and
snug. I like
listening to
her talk.

I want
Mommy!

My first smiles

I'm growing bigger and stronger. I can kick and wave my arms around. And I am getting to know my family. When I see them, I give them a big smile.

I am six weeks old now and growing fast. Mommy feeds me milk whenever I'm hungry.

This is my brother Sam. He's three years old. He talks to me and makes funny faces to try to make me smile.

I'm growing fast

Daddy is holding me. Look how I've grown. I can almost keep my head up now, but it is still a bit wobbly. I can laugh, too, and make cooing noises like a dove. Coo!

I am getting plumper and my hair has grown. My hands look really tiny next to Daddy's.

I am four months old. I can roll over onto my tummy now.

I like to be propped
up in a seat so I
can watch what
is going on.

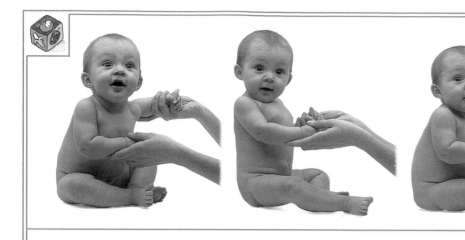

My new skills

I can pick up toys and hold on to them now. My favorite game is trying to sit up. Also, I have started eating real food from a spoon.

At six months, I'm nearly as big as my toy basket.

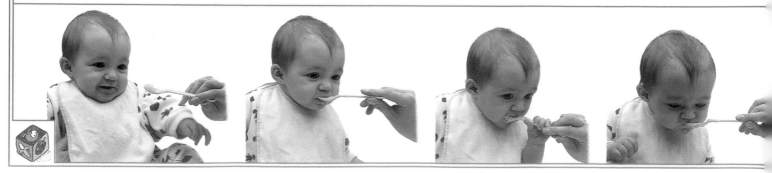

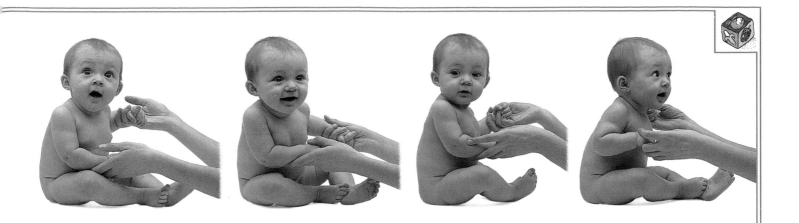

I can kick my legs really high and sometimes even suck my toes. When I do, everyone laughs.

I can sit up

I am eight months old and can sit up all by myself. I sit on the floor and play with my toys.

Look at my basket! I can do lots of tricks with it. I'll try to climb into it.

Maybe I can build something with these blocks. Oops, too heavy!

What about these hoops? That didn't work – I'll just have to try again.

I can crawl

At last I can crawl and go exploring. When I see a toy I want, I can go and get it. And if the toy is on a chair, I'll stand up to reach it.

I am ten months old. I can just peep over the back of my chair.

There! Got the ball. I can only stand up if I hold on to something. It's really hard. My legs feel a bit shaky.

It's my bathtime

I can do lots of things on my own now, but I still need help. Mommy has to wash me and get me dressed.

I don't like having my hair washed. When it's over, I'm wrapped up snugly in a towel.

I am one year old now and can stand up without holding on!

I can talk

I learn a lot from my brother Sam. I talk to him all the time, but he doesn't understand me.

I'm bigger than my basket, but still smaller than Sam.

I wonder if I can do that? I watch Sam carefully and copy what he does. That's how I learn new tricks.

I can say three real words – "dog," "duck," and "Dow." That's my special name for Sam.

I can walk

Look at me! I can walk all on my own. I have bare feet so I won't slip, and I hold my arms out to help me balance. Soon I will have my first pair of real shoes.

I am
fourteen
months
old now.

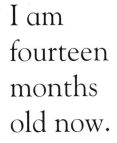

I carry my bear when I
walk, but drop him if
I see my toy phone.
I chatter all the
time in my own
baby talk.

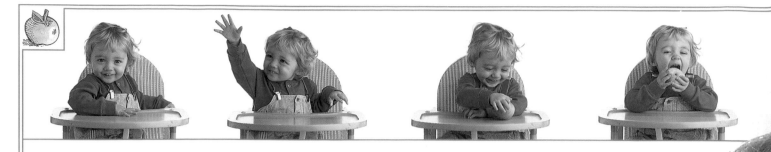

I can feed myself

I don't need anyone to feed me anymore. I will eat just about anything as long as it tastes nice. I can use a sipper cup and eat with a spoon, but I still use my fingers a lot. I make a real mess!

I am fifteen months old now and twice as big as my basket.

All gone! That was delicious.
Maybe there's more hiding
under my bowl . . .

Here I go

I want to try to ride the trike. It was Sam's and he still likes playing with it. Maybe he'll let me have a turn.

I am sixteen months old now.

That's good. It's just the right size for me.

If I'm quick, will I be able to ride away before Sam sees me?

It's not that easy to balance on one leg.

Off I go! Sam will never be able to catch me now.

Look at me!

I'm really growing fast and now look more like a little girl than a baby. I like dressing up and my basket is full of funny hats, huge shoes, and colored beads that Mommy doesn't wear anymore.

Look at this necklace. I'm going to try on all the beads. Kangaroo is going to as well.

I am one and a half years old now.

See how I've grown

Here you can see how much I have changed as I've grown.

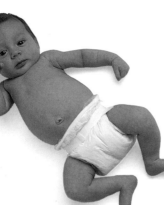

When I was six months old I could kick really high.

Here I am six weeks old.

Here I was four days old. I spent most of my time asleep.

At ten months old I could crawl.

Then I learned to stand up.

I am fourteen months old here.

Now I am one and
a half years old and
can do lots of things
on my own. I'm not
a baby anymore!

Here I am
eight months old.

By the time I was sixteen
months old, I could ride a trike.

 hello!

First words
These are the very first
words I learned to say.

 bye-bye!

apple

drink

book

socks

shoes

car

dog

duck

cat